V&A Pattern
The Fifties

V&A Publishing

V&A Pattern
The Fifties

First published by V&A Publishing, 2009
V&A Publishing
Victoria and Albert Museum
South Kensington
London SW7 2RL
www.vandapublishing.com

Distributed in North America by Harry N. Abrams Inc., New York
© The Board of Trustees of the Victoria and Albert Museum, 2009

The moral right of the author has been asserted.

ISBN 978 1 85177 585 9
Library of Congress Control Number 2009923088

14 13 12 11 10 9 8 7 6 5
2018 2017 2016 2015 2014

A catalogue record for this book is available
from the British Library.

Design: Rose

Front cover illustration (A):
Lucienne Day/Heal's
Small Hours, furnishing fabric. Screen-printed linen. UK, 1952 (V&A: CIRC.58–1953)
Pages 2–3 (B):
Joan Miró/Fuller Fabrics
Woman and Birds, furnishing fabric. Screen-printed linen. USA, 1956
(V&A. CIRC.455–1956)
Page 6 (C):
Robert Stewart/Liberty & Co.
Macrahanish, furnishing fabric. Printed fabric. UK, 1954 (V&A: CIRC.492–1954)
Page 11 (D):
Palladio Wallpapers
Bistro, wallpaper sample (from a pattern book). UK, 1955 (V&A: E.444:75–1988)
Pages 78–9 (E):
Roger Nicholson/David Whitehead Ltd
Furnishing fabric. Printed. UK, 1951 (V&A: CIRC.284–1951)

Letters (in brackets) refer to the file name of the
images on the accompanying disc.

Printed in China

V&A Publishing

Supporting the world's leading
museum of art and design,
the Victoria and Albert
Museum, London

V&A Pattern

Each *V&A Pattern* book is an introduction to the Victoria and Albert Museum's extraordinarily diverse design archives. The museum has more than three million designs for textiles, decorations, wallpapers and prints; some well-known, others less so. This series explores pattern-making in all its forms, across the world and through the centuries. The books are intended to be both beautiful and useful – showing patterns to enjoy in their own right and as inspiration for new design.

V&A Pattern presents the greatest names and styles in design, while also highlighting the work of anonymous draughtsmen and designers, often working unacknowledged in workshops, studios and factories, and responsible for designs of aesthetic originality and technical virtuosity. Many of the most interesting and imaginative designs are seen too rarely. *V&A Pattern* gathers hidden treasures – from pattern books, swatch books, company archives, design records and catalogues – to form a fascinating introduction to the variety and beauty of pattern at the V&A.

The compact disc at the back of each book invites you to appreciate the ingenuity of the designs, and the endless possibilities for their application. To use the images professionally, you need permission from V&A Images, as the V&A controls – on behalf of others – the rights held in its books and CD-Roms. *V&A Pattern* can only ever be a tiny selection of the designs available at www.vandaimages.com. We see requests to use images as an opportunity to help us to develop and improve our licensing programme – and for us to let you know about images you may not have found elsewhere.

The Fifties
Pattern, colour
and creativity
Sue Prichard

The patterns illustrated in this book are from the Victoria and Albert Museum's textile and wallpaper collections. They are representative of some of the most inventive and innovative pattern designs produced during the twentieth century. The extraordinary quantity and variety of textiles and wallpapers acquired by intuitive and proactive curators pay tribute to some of the most dynamic artists, designers and manufacturers of the 1950s.

The period is dominated by what is commonly defined as the 'contemporary' style. Often imitated, exuberant patterns and bright colourways have ensured each work's place in the lexicon of both British and international design history. The emerging trend for abstraction in the fine arts acted as a stimulus for many European and American designers. The fluid organic forms employed by Joan Miro and Paul Klee, and the brightly coloured mobiles created by Alexander Calder, are evident in the imaginative and inventive patterns created for fabrics and wallpapers. These seemingly casual, effortless designs are often described as 'whimsical'; however, such inventive combinations owe much to the rigorous art school training of new and established designers.

The ubiquitous floral tradition, the mainstay of the British textile industry since the last century, was revitalized and reinvented during the 1950s. The overblown flowers and blooms beloved by the Edwardians were replaced by more fundamental plant forms. Skeletal twigs, stems, leaves and seed heads were popular motifs, formally arranged along grid lines, referencing a more disciplined and architectural approach to pattern design. As the decade progressed, the contemporary style continued to evolve. Delicate doodle-like compositions were replaced by large scale repeats more suited to open plan areas of corporate and public buildings.

The Festival of Britain provided the visual platform for new designs by some of the country's most talented designers. The groundbreaking combination of exciting and original designs with bold colour contrasts caught the public's imagination. The spindly patterns of the contemporary style were acknowledged internationally, winning awards both in Europe and America. Equally adventurous but less commercially popular, the range of designs based on crystal structure diagrams illustrate the willingness of the newly formed Council of Industrial Design (CoID) to create a dialogue between different disciplines, focusing on new scientific discoveries. The CoID also emphasized the project's antecedents: 'these crystal structure diagrams had the discipline of exact repetitive symmetry; they were above all very pretty and were full of rich variety; ... they were essentially modern because the technique that constructed them was quite recent, and yet, like all successful decoration of the past, they derived from nature – although it was nature at a sub microscopic scale not previously revealed' (*Design*, no. 29–30, 1951). The brief captured the public's imagination and the striking interpretations of amoebic shapes appeared on a eclectic range of dress and furnishing fabrics, ceramics, wallpaper and glass.

The role of British manufacturers in commissioning and supporting young, talented designers contributed to the climate of experimentation and innovation. Enlightened individuals such as Tom Worthington (at Heal's) and John Murry (for David Whitehead Ltd) encouraged fruitful and productive collaborations free from stylistic or technical limitations. The bold and progressive design policies of textile firms including Heal's, Liberty's, British Celanese and David Whiteheads were recognized by the CoID who stated that such commissions were 'a welcome reminder' of the country's tradition of experimentation. Wallpaper manufacturers were equally adventurous; Cole & Son, John Line and the Wall Paper Manufacturers Ltd (WLM) all commissioned leading artists and designers, launching 'contemporary' limited edition ranges. The intelligent application of advanced screen-printing techniques and both natural and man-made fabrics contributed enormously to the translation of exuberant and vibrant designs into mass production. The contemporary style thus became not only desirable but also affordable, while quality control ensured that 'cheap need not be cheap and nasty'.

The alignment of fine and applied art disciplines in the 1950s produced a variety of consumer goods both attractive and accessible to homeowners keen to put the austerity of the war years behind them. The combination of unrestricted free-form patterns and vibrant colours reflected the optimism of this new 'Elizabethan Age', heralding a new approach to domestic decoration. The constraints of the previous decade, economic and social, paved the way for a more urbane and relaxed approach to modern living, without the historicism of the past. Pattern could be used to accent an architectural feature, or combined in stunning contrasts. The emphasis on a lighter touch, underpinned by a willingness to embrace new sources of inspiration, testifies to the vision and talent of post-war designers, artists and manufacturers, a vision that continues to resonate well into the twenty-first century.

1
Margaret Cooper
Furnishing fabric. Screen-printed cotton. UK, 1950 (V&A: CIRC.233–1950)

2
Barbara Pile
Furnishing fabric. Screen-printed linen. UK, 1950 (V&A: CIRC.232–1950)

3
Terence Conran/David Whitehead Ltd
Furnishing fabric. Screen-printed cotton. UK, 1950 (V&A: CIRC.503–1953)

4
Sylvia Priestley/John Line & Sons Ltd
Early Bird, wallpaper. Screen-printed paper. UK, 1951 (V&A: E.887–1978)

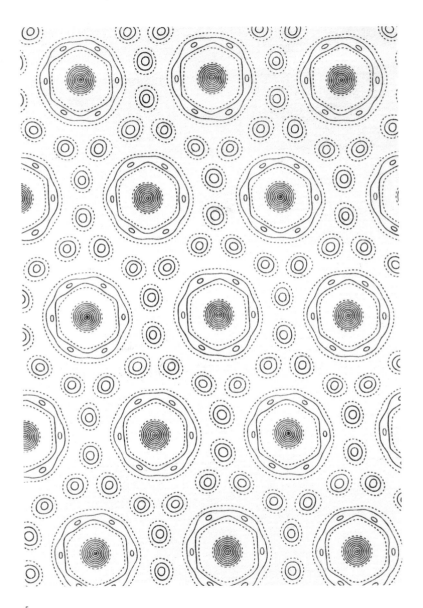

5
Barlow & Jones Ltd
Haemoglobin, dress fabric. Roller-printed cotton. UK, 1951 (V&A: CIRC. 77–1968)

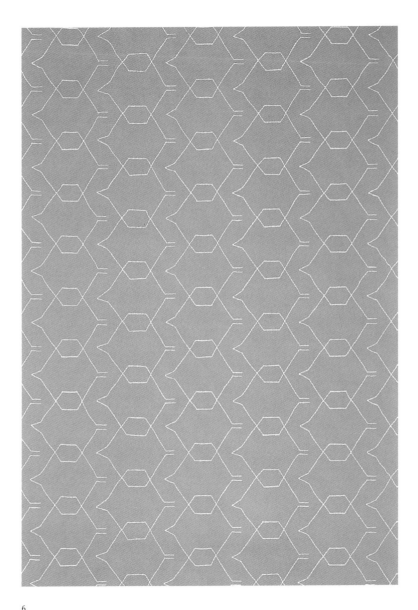

6
Folke Sundberg/Engblads Tapetfabrik
Alle, wallpaper sample. Screen-printed paper. Sweden, 1953 (V&A: E.578–1966)

7
Frank Lloyd Wright/F. Schumacher & Co.
Design 706, wallpaper. Screen-printed paper. USA, 1956 (V&A: E.582–1966)

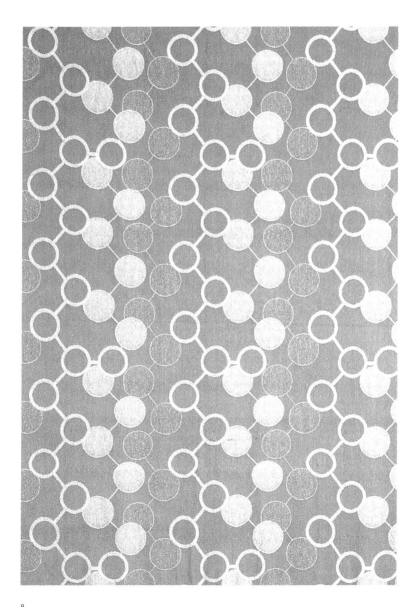

8
Marianne Straub/Warner & Sons Ltd
Helmsley, furnishing fabric. Woven cotton. UK, 1951 (V&A: CIRC.308–1951)

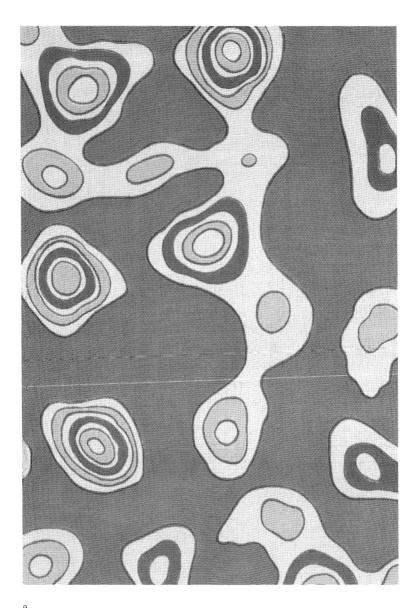

9
S.M. Slade/British Celanese Ltd
Afwillite 8.45, furnishing fabric (see also plate 10). Screen-printed rayon. UK, c.1951 (V&A: CIRC.75A–1968)

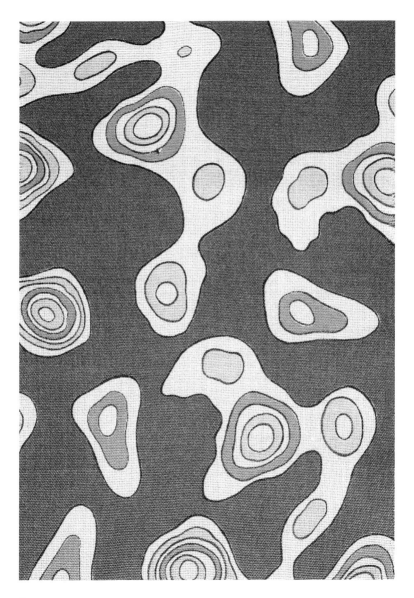

10
S.M. Slade/British Celanese Ltd
Afwillite 8.45, furnishing fabric (see also plate 9). Screen-printed rayon. UK, c.1951 (V&A: CIRC.75C–1968)

11
Marianne Straub/Warner & Sons
Surrey, furnishing fabric. Jacquard woven wool, cotton and rayon. UK, 1951 (V&A: CIRC.306–1951)

12
Robert Sevant/John Line & Sons Ltd
8.25 Insulin, wallpaper. Screen-printed paper. UK, 1951 (V&A: E.888–1978)

13
Lucienne Day/Heal's
Calyx, furnishing fabric. Screen-printed linen. UK, 1951 (V&A: CIRC.190–1954)

14
Terence Conran/David Whitehead Ltd
Chequers, furnishing fabric. Screen-printed cotton. UK, 1951 (V&A: CIRC.283–1951)

15
Bent Karlby/DahlsTapetfabrik
Haelderne, wallpaper. Block-printed paper. Denmark, 1951 (V&A: E.897–1979)

16
Jacqueline Groag/John Line & Sons Ltd
Isabella, wallpaper. Block-printed paper. UK, 1951 (V&A: E.880–1978)

17
Mary Oliver/Gayonnes Ltd
Porto Fino, furnishing fabric. Screen-printed cotton. UK, 1952 (V&A: CIRC.62–1953)

18

John Barker/David Whitehead Ltd
Festival of Britain, furnishing fabric. Screen-printed rayon satin. UK, 1951 (V&A: T. 288–1982)

Palladio Wallpapers
Malaga, wallpaper sample (from a pattern book). UK, 1955 (V&A: E.444:21–1988)

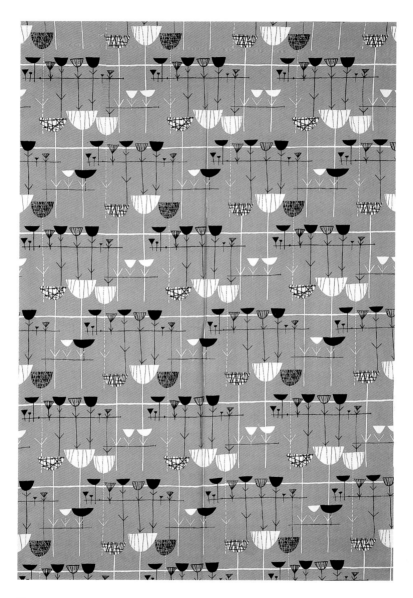

20
Marion Mahler/David Whitehead Ltd
Furnishing fabric. Screen-printed cotton. UK, 1952 (V&A: CIRC.14–1953)

21
Marion Mahler/David Whitehead Ltd
Furnishing fabric. Screen-printed cotton crepe. UK, 1952 (V&A: CIRC.8–1953)

22
Marian Mahler/David Whitehead Ltd
Curtain fabric. Screen-printed cotton. UK, 1950 (V&A: T.504:2–1996)

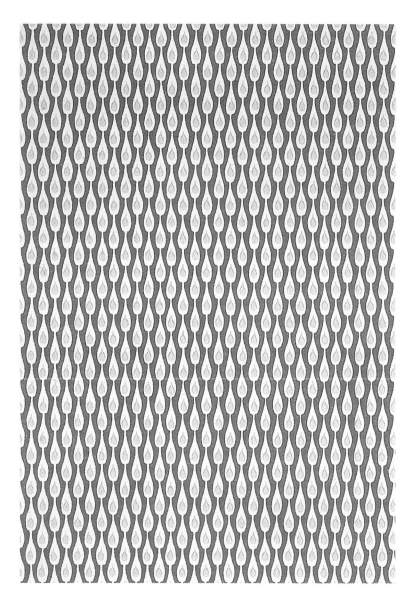

23
Preben Dahlstrom/Dahls tapetfabrik
Ljus i Flaske (Light in Bottles), wallpaper sample. Block-printed paper. Denmark, 1956 (V&A: E.568–1966)

24
Cuno Fischer / Weberei Frittlingen, Alber & Co
Blues, furnishing fabric. Printed cotton. Germany, 1955 (V&A: CIRC.216–1955)

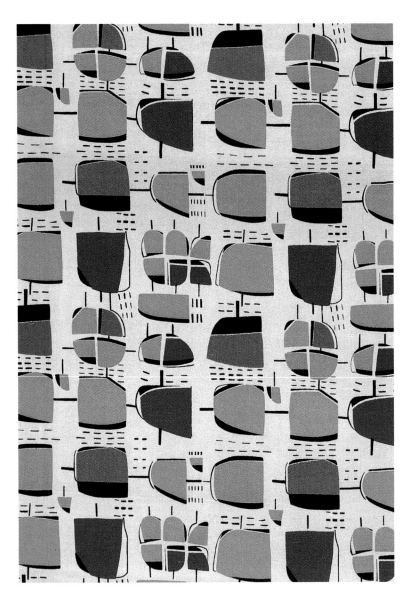

25
Jacqueline Groag/David Whitehead Ltd
Furnishing fabric. Roller-printed spun rayon. UK, 1952 (V&A: CIRC.12–1953)

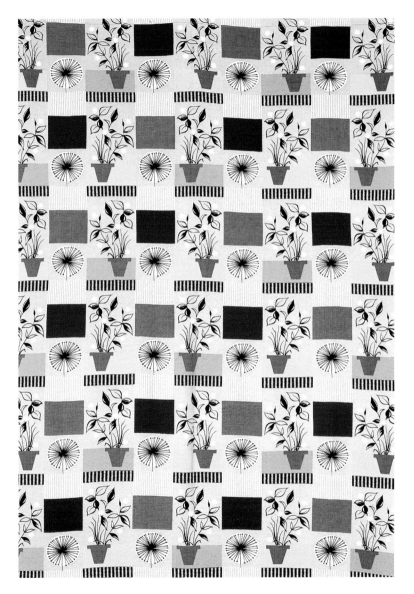

26
Tom Mellors / David Whitehead Ltd
Flowerpots, furnishing fabric. Roller-printed spun rayon. UK, 1954 (V&A: CIRC.506–1954)

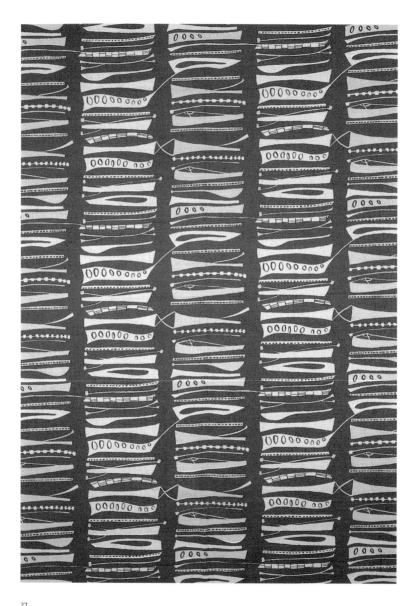

27
Lucienne Day/Edinburgh Weavers
Foreshore, furnishing fabric. Screen-printed cotton. UK, 1952 (V&A: CIRC.143–1953)

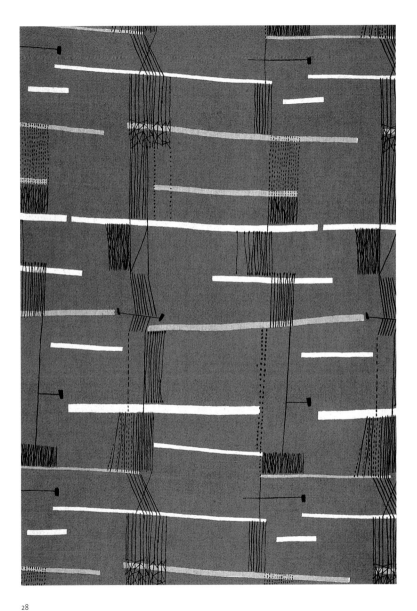

28
Lucienne Day/Heal's
Springboard, furnishing fabric. Screen-printed linen. UK, 1954 (V&A: CIRC.209–1954)

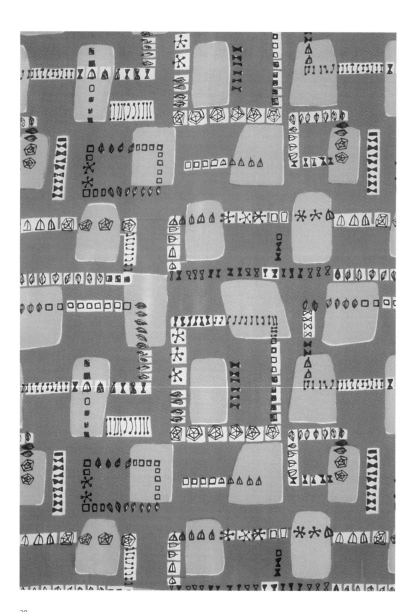

Lucienne Day/British Celanese Ltd
Quadrille, furnishing fabric. Printed rayon taffeta. UK, 1953 (V&A: CIRC.382–1953)

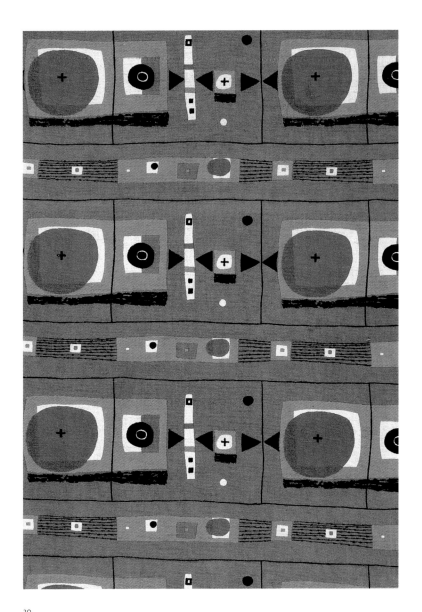

30
Robert Stewart/Liberty & Co.
Applecross, furnishing fabric. Screen-printed linen. UK, 1954 (V&A: CIRC.484–1954)

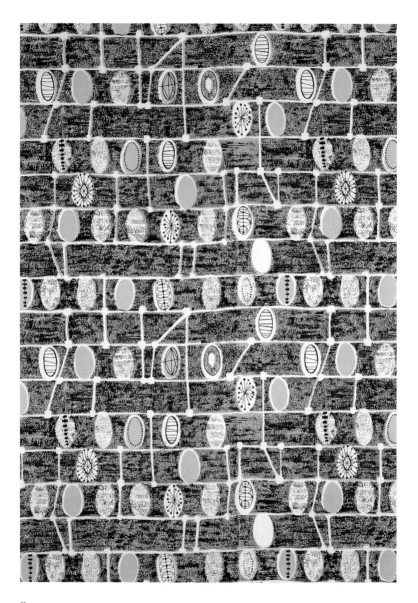

31
Lucienne Day/Heal's
Strata, furnishing fabric. Screen-printed cotton. UK, 1952 (V&A: CIRC.52–1953)

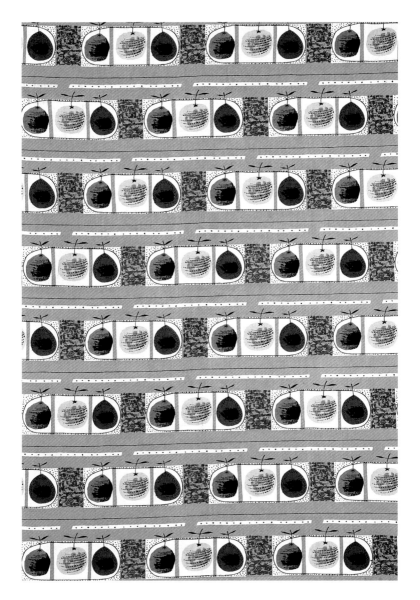

32
Robert Stewart/Liberty & Co.
Kier, furnishing fabric. Screen-printed linen. UK, 1954 (V&A: CIRC.483–1954)

33
Gigi Tessari/Manifattura JSA
Spago, furnishing fabric. Screen-printed cotton and spun rayon. Italy, 1957 (V&A: CIRC.200–1957)

34
Pablo Picasso/Fuller Fabrics
Furnishing fabric. Screen-printed cotton. USA, 1956 (V&A: CIRC.449–1956)

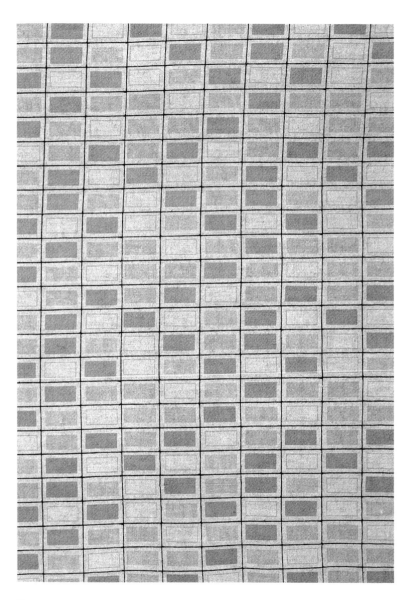

35
Angelo Testa/F. Schumacher & Co.
Square Deal, furnishing fabric. Printed linen. USA, 1954 (V&A: CIRC.117–1954)

36
Peter Shuttleworth/Lightbown Aspinall
Toccata, wallpaper sample. Screen-printed paper. UK, *c*.1952. (V&A: E.958–1978)

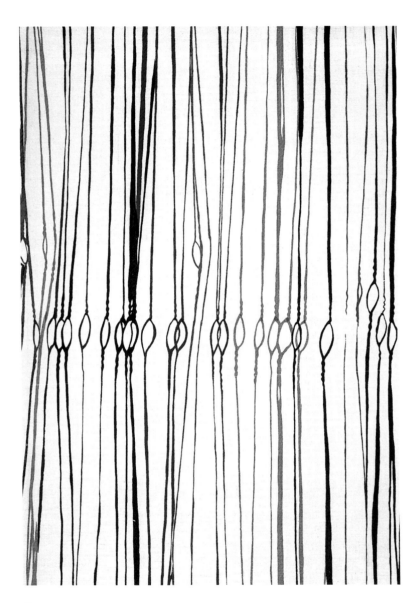

37
Eszter Haraszty/Knoll Textiles Inc.
Fibra, furnishing fabric. Printed linen. USA, 1953 (V&A: CIRC.141–1954)

Lucienne Day/British Celanese Ltd
Palisade, furnishing fabric. Printed rayon taffeta. UK, 1953 (V&A: CIRC.384–1953)

39
Robert Nicholson/Palladio Wallpapers
Collonade, wallpaper sample (from a pattern book, see also plate 40). UK, 1955 (V&A: E.444:69–1988)

40
Robert Nicholson/Palladio Wallpapers
Colonnade, wallpaper sample (from a pattern book, see also plate 39). UK, 1955 (V&A: E.444:68–1988)

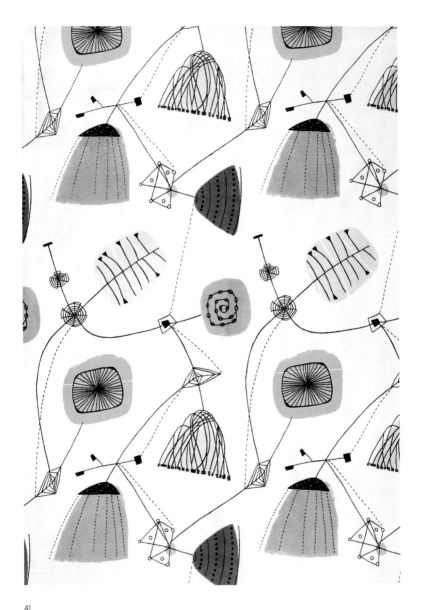

41
Lucienne Day/British Celanese Ltd
Perpetua, furnishing fabric. Screen-printed rayon. UK, 1953 (V&A: CIRC.385–1953)

42
Lucienne Day/Heal's
Small Hours, furnishing fabric. Screen-printed linen. UK, 1952 (V&A: CIRC.58–1953)

43
Sylvia Chalmers/Elizabeth Eaton Ltd
Feathered Friends, furnishing fabric. Screen-printed cotton. UK, 1953 (V&A: CIRC.174–1954)

44
John Drummond/Anne Loosely
Piscatore, furnishing fabric. Screen-printed cotton satin. UK, 1953 (V&A: CIRC.405–1953)

45
Lucienne Day/Heal's
Graphica, furnishing fabric. Screen-printed cotton. UK, 1954 (V&A: CIRC.211–1954)

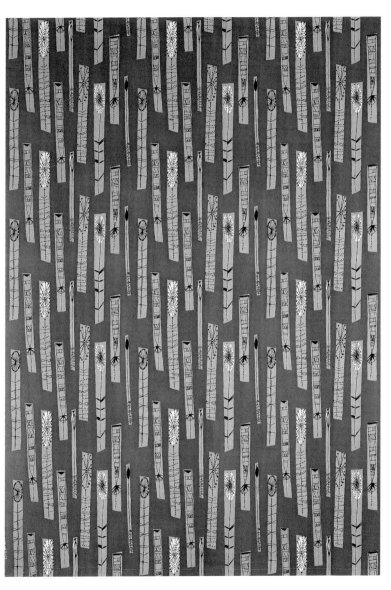

46
Lucienne Day/Heal's
Flower Show, furnishing fabric. Screen-printed cotton. UK, 1954 (V&A: CIRC.201–1954)

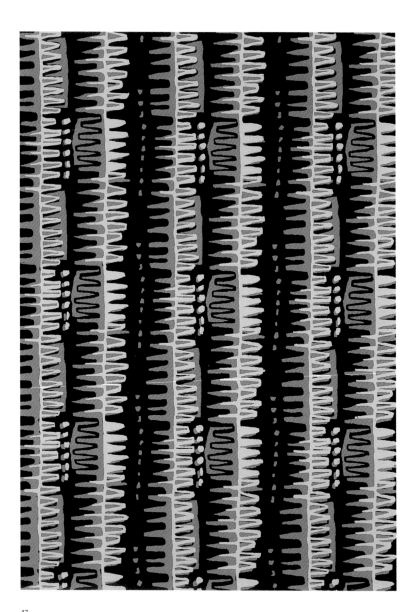

47
Edward Hughes/Palladio Wallpapers
Basuto, wallpaper sample (from a pattern book). UK, 1955 (V&A: E.444:17–1988)

48
Jacqueline Groag/Liberty & Co.
Books, furnishing fabric. Screen-printed linen. UK, 1954 (V&A: CIRC.490–1954)

49
Lucienne Day/Heal's
Isosceles, furnishing fabric. Screen-printed cotton. UK, 1955 (V&A: CIRC.473–1956)

50
John Drummond/Wemyss Weavecraft Ltd
Dovedale, furnishing fabric. Screen-printed linen. UK, 1953 (V&A: CIRC.372–1953)

51
Sylvia Chalmers/Heal's
Jaborandi, furnishing fabric. Screen-printed linen. UK, 1953 (V&A: CIRC.55–1953)

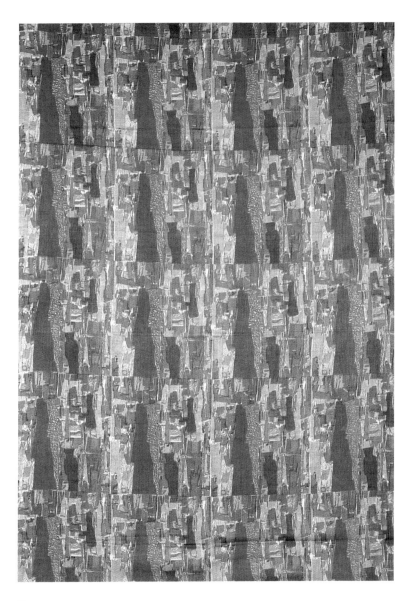

52
Sara Provan/Konwiser Inc.
Capriccio, furnishing fabric. Printed cotton. USA, 1954 (V&A: CIRC.178–1954)

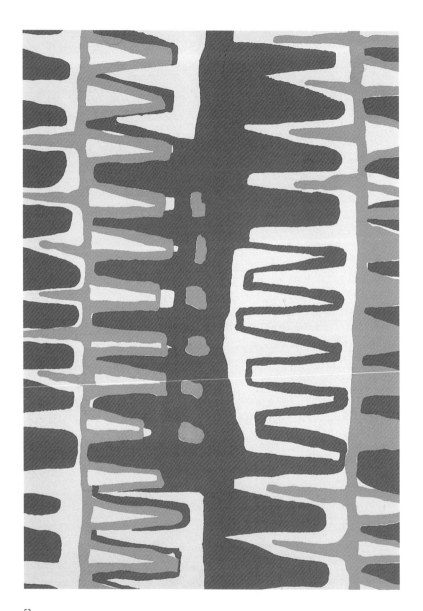

Edward Hughes/Palladio Wallpapers
Basuto, wallpaper sample (from a pattern book). UK, 1955 (V&A: E.444:19–1988)

Palladio Wallpapers
Polonaise, wallpaper sample (from a pattern book). UK, 1955 (V&A: E.444:31–1988)

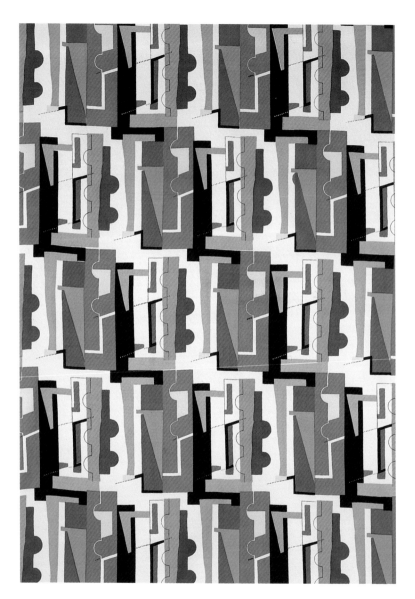

55
John Piper/David Whitehead Ltd
Heads, furnishing fabric. Screen-printed rayon. UK, 1956 (V&A: CIRC.641–1956)

56
Ruth Adler/Adler Schnee Associates
Keys, printed hair cloth. USA, 1954 (V&A: CIRC.499–1954)

57
Joan Miró/Fuller Fabrics
Dancing People, furnishing fabric. Screen-printed cotton. USA, 1956 (V&A: CIRC.441–1956)

58
Joan Miró/Fuller Fabrics
People & Birds, furnishing fabric, screen-printed cotton. USA, 1956 (V&A: CIRC.442–1956)

Lucienne Day/John Line & Sons Ltd
Provence, wallpaper. Screen-printed paper. UK, 1951 (V&A: E.569–1966)

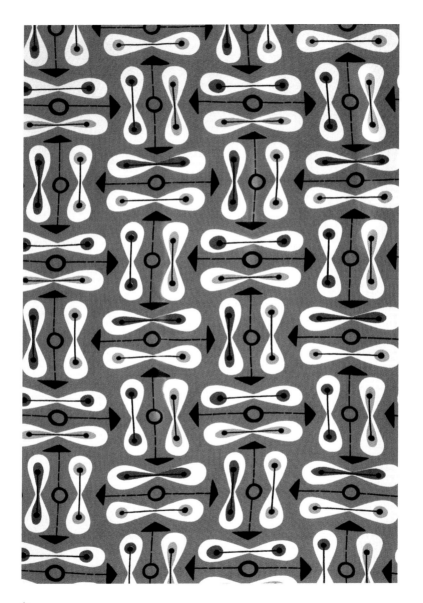

60
J. Feldman/David Whitehead Ltd
Furnishing fabric. Roller-printed spun rayon. UK, 1954 (V&A: CIRC.504–1954)

Lucienne Day/Heal's
Forest, furnishing fabric. Roller-printed cotton. UK, 1959 (V&A: CIRC.37–1959)

62
Shinkichi Tajiri/Rasch & Co.
Louisiana, wallpaper. Machine printed paper. Germany, c.1955 (V&A: E.972–1978)

63
Mary Harper/Edinburgh Weavers
Pallida, furnishing fabric. Screen-printed glazed cotton. UK, 1958 (V&A: CIRC.232–1958)

64
Robert Dodd/Heal's
Rosa Bella, furnishing fabric. Screen-printed cotton satin. UK, 1959 (V&A: CIRC.163–1959)

65
Hilda Durkin/Heal's
Village Church, furnishing fabric. Screen-printed cotton. UK, 1954 (V&A: CIRC.212–1954)

66
Robert Nicholson/Palladio Wallpapers
Columns, wallpaper sample (from a pattern book). UK, 1955 (V&A: E.444:13–1988)

Further Reading

Conran, Terence
Printed Textile Design
London, 1957

Feldman, Anita, ed.
Henry Moore Textiles
London, 2008

Halford, Lucy
Colour Rules Your Home
London & New York, 1958

Harris, Jennifer
Lucienne Day:
A career in design
Manchester, 1993

Ikoku, Ngozi
British Textile Design
from 1940 to the present
London, 1999

Ikoku, Ngozi, ed.
Post-war British Textiles
London 2002

Jackson, Lesley
Robin & Lucienne Day:
Pioneers of Contemporary Design
London, 2001

Jackson, Lesley
Twentieth Century Pattern
Design: Textile &
Wallpaper Pioneers
London, 2002

Jackson, Lesley
From Atoms to Patterns: Crystal
Structure Designs from the 1951
Festival of Britain
London, 2008

MacCarthy, F.
All Things Bright & Beautiful.
Design in Britain 1830 to Today
London, 1972

Raynor, G., Chamberlain, R.
and Stapleton, A.,
Artists' Textiles in Britain
1945–1970: a Democratic
Art, Woodbridge, 2003

Digital Images

The patterns reproduced in this book are stored on the
accompanying compact disc as jpeg files (at approximately
A5-size, 300 dpi). You should be able to open them, and
manipulate them, direct from the CD-ROM in most modern
image software (on Windows or Mac platforms), and no
installation should be required (although we, as publishers,
cannot guarantee absolutely that the disc will be accessible
for every computer).

Instructions for tracing and tiling the images will be found
with the documentation for your software.

The names of the files correspond to the V&A inventory
numbers of the images.

Copyright